This book is dedicated to all who find Nature not an adversary to conquer and destroy, but a storehouse of infinite knowledge and experience linking man to all things past and present. They know conserving the natural environment is essential to our future well being.

MESA VERDE
THE STORY BEHIND THE SCENERY®

by Linda Martin

Linda Martin, "a farm girl from Nebraska," is a graduate of Creighton University. A career National Park Service employee, Linda has spent 17 years working in Mesa Verde National Park. In this book she shares the intimate knowledge she has gained by roaming the canyons and exploring the hidden recesses of the Four Corners area.

Mesa Verde National Park, located in southwestern Colorado, was established in 1906 to safeguard the most notable and best-preserved cliff dwellings and other works of a prehistoric culture in the United States.

Front cover: Cliff Palace, photo by Grant Heilman. Inside front cover: Interior of Spruce Tree House, photo by George H. H. Huey. Page 1: Cliff Palace Tower, photo by Robert Nowak. Pages 2/3: Long House on Wetherill Mesa, photo by Tom Till.

Edited by Mary L. Van Camp. Book design by K. C. DenDooven.

Third Printing, 1995.

MESA VERDE: THE STORY BEHIND THE SCENERY® © 1993 KC PUBLICATIONS, INC.
LC 93-77024. ISBN 0-88714-075-0.

Nature in Mesa Verde is like an artist capturing a cliff dwelling image or mood and preserving it for posterity. The sky casts a glow on the pinkish-brown sandstone walls, fading into a shadowy luminescence as sunset approaches.

The Mesa Verde plateau glimmers in sunlight most of the year, inviting people and animals to take advantage of the lush tabletop and canyon environments. Although most visitors arrive looking for the cliff dwellings they have read about in school, many are surprised at the variety of vegetation and wildlife awaiting them. It is little wonder that the Anasazi settled here hundreds of years ago. The prolific natural setting allowed them to prosper for centuries. Life was secure enough that they concentrated part of their time skillfully crafting pottery, jewelry, baskets, and stone tools. They developed elaborate religious rituals still carried on by Pueblo descendants today. Their architectural achievements were amazing for a stone-age people. Mesa Verde is a living legacy of people and nature working in harmony with each other.

Snow dots the walls of Far View House, a prominent mesa-top site offering panoramic views of the surrounding countryside.

It is frustrating for some visitors that so many questions about the Anasazi remain unanswered. Maybe the lack of written history is actually a bonus, forcing us to use our imaginations and conjure up our own theories.

The Anasazi Legacy

Cliff dwellings—ancient stone houses nestled in cliff alcoves and somehow shrouded in mystery—are almost synonymous with Mesa Verde National Park. Visitors inevitably want to see Cliff Palace with its towering walls and majestic setting. They marvel at the ingenuity of prehistoric people who were able to create such architectural wonders. Yet the cliff dwellings are only a small part of the entire Mesa Verde story. They represent only the last 75-100 years of a civilization that spanned centuries. Who were these people? What brought them to this area? Why did they leave? These are the questions surrounding Mesa Verde and its prehistoric culture.

It is frustrating for some visitors that so many questions about the Anasazi remain unanswered. As a group, Americans are used to definite answers, expecting that scientific knowledge can unravel anything. Maybe the lack of written history is actually a bonus, forcing us to use our imaginations and conjure up our own theories based on known facts about why the cliff dwellings were built and what happened to the people.

The earliest inhabitants of the Mesa Verde area arrived around 10,000 years ago. They made a living hunting wild animals and collecting native plant foods. Archaeologists know some details about these people, although they left few remnants of their nomadic existence. After several thousand years of hunting and gathering, they began adopting a more settled lifestyle.

▷ **A steady stream of visitors strolls through** Cliff Palace during the summer months. The sound of their voices echoing off the rock must be reminiscent of Anasazi activity in the 1200s.

◁ **Adults and children alike delight in climbing** down the ladder into a Spruce Tree House kiva. The base of the ladder rests near the firepit, and smoke wafting out the opening may have been a cleansing or purification rite for the Anasazi.

This transition emerged because of two major factors: the building of permanent living and storage structures, and the cultivation of a garden (horticulture) and domestication of plants. Once people began leading an agricultural way of life, changes in their cultural and social habits soon followed. In the Four Corners area of the southwestern United States this way of life was called the Anasazi cultural tradition.

Who Were The Anasazi?

Anasazi is a Navajo Indian word meaning "ancient ones." There is no record of what the Anasazi called themselves. For that matter, based upon the artifacts and other information removed from Mesa Verde sites, archaeologists have an incomplete understanding of Anasazi social, political, or religious practices and little data about their abstract beliefs.

When they left this area, the Anasazi migrated south into what is now New Mexico and Arizona, settling in the Rio Grande pueblos, Acoma, Zuni, and the Hopi mesas. Over the years their descendants assimilated into these groups. For this reason archaeologists use modern Pueblo practices to help analyze archaeological sites and answer questions about them. Rangers remind visitors of this when they take a tour of a dwelling.

▲ **Anasazi farmers cut the pinyon pine and juniper** trees on the mesa top to establish fields where they grew corn, beans, and squash. The growing season of around 150 days and the fertile soil produced healthy crops except for extremely dry years. Corn was a dietary staple and must have been eaten with most meals.

Modern Pueblo society is often clan oriented, consisting of related families descended from common ancestors. Unlike Europeans, who trace their ancestry through their father's side of the family (patrilineal), most Pueblos trace their line of descent through the women (matrilineal). Anasazi families were also probably matrilineal with women owning the houses as well as the property inside them. When a couple married,

◄ **The reconstructed pit house in Step House clearly** illustrates roof construction during Modified Basket Maker times. A thick layer of mud on the outside helped insulate against the elements, keeping people dry and fairly cozy.

the man moved into his wife's house and joined her relatives.

Similar customs applied to religious and ceremonial activities. Important elements in their lives revolved around hunting, farming in a fairly marginal environment, and praying for rain and fertility. Their gods must have made sure that plants, animals, and water were available for daily existence. These are important concepts to keep in mind when considering the Mesa Verde Anasazi.

There are always visitor questions about the size of the Anasazi and how long they lived. An average man was 5'4" to 5'5" tall, while an average woman was 5' to 5'1". Burials reveal that they had straight black hair, often cropped short for the women. They had muscular bodies adapted to the vigorous activity of their daily lives. An average lifespan was fairly short—about 32-34 years—although some people lived into their 40s and 50s. Infant mortality was high; about 50 percent of the children died before they reached the age of five. Women typically lived shorter lives than men because of child-bearing difficulties. These statistics seem strange to visitors, yet Europeans of that time period averaged the same size and lived about the same length of time.

Causes of death for the Anasazi ranged from arthritis and rheumatism to poor sanitary conditions and tooth decay. Skeletal remains often show teeth worn to the nub from chewing, or a lack of teeth completely. Such people may have pulled cavity-ridden teeth to eliminate pain and suffering. Dietary deficiencies such as iron were common. Some people endured bone deformities which made movement painful. All of these difficulties were typical considering the type of lifestyle they led.

THE BASKET MAKER TRADITION

Because the earliest Anasazi excelled in the art of basketry, they are known as "Basket Makers." Many of their baskets were so finely woven that they would hold water. They also wove intricate sandals made of yucca fibers. The Basket Makers hunted with a throwing spear called an atlatl, and gathered seeds, nuts, and berries. They often lived in shallow rock shelters where they stored food in stone-lined cysts. Archaeologists have not located any early Basket Maker sites in the park.

By A.D. 550, the Modified Basket Maker Period began, coinciding with Mesa Verde occupation in cliff alcoves and on the mesa top.

▲ **T-shaped doorways are a common feature in cliff** dwelling architecture. They are usually found in walls that border courtyards. They may have served a practical purpose, making movement in and out of a room easier, or the "T" shape may have had some symbolic meaning to the Anasazi.

Modified Basket Makers continued to make baskets, but they learned a new concept vital to their cultural development—the making of pottery. Pottery made food processing and cooking not only easier, but also more efficient.

The Anasazi built semi-subterranean dwellings called pit houses on the mesa top and in alcoves. Agriculture developed with the growth of corn, beans, and squash, the three staple crops of the Southwest. They replaced the atlatl with the bow and arrow, allowing them to hunt with greater efficiency. They domesticated turkeys, using them as a source of food and feathers. Although pit-house sites are not as impressive as cliff dwellings, this period laid the foundations for the flourishing farming tradition which visitors find so remarkable today.

▲ **Cliff alcoves were cold and miserable places during the winter months, when days were short and** *temperatures dropped to zero or below overnight. Snowstorms made movement difficult, yet examples of Anasazi snowshoes exist. Perhaps the kivas were favorite places to sleep during long winter nights. It is easy to imagine people telling stories while huddled around the firepit in these snug, underground rooms.*

Pueblo Occupation

Around A.D. 750, the Anasazi began replacing their pit houses with surface dwellings, and a new era in construction began. The Developmental Pueblo Period is characterized by rows of connected rooms with vertical walls and flat roofs. In front of these L- or U-shaped houses the Anasazi dug deep pit rooms, separating the architectural structure into an above-ground and a below-ground unit.

The underground rooms later evolved into ceremonial structures known by the Hopi word "kiva." Surface houses developed into masonry units using sandstone blocks and mud mortar. These architectural achievements signaled that a more formalized kinship and religious system had evolved.

One interesting aspect of Developmental Pueblo living was the change in cradleboards. They were soft and padded in the Modified Basket Maker Period, protecting the infant's head. In contrast, the new cradleboards were hard, causing a flattening of the baby's head and broadening of the face. Who knows—maybe fashion-conscious Anasazi thought this made them more beautiful!

Pottery-making techniques continued to improve throughout the Developmental Pueblo Period. In fact, pottery analysis is one way archaeologists can date Anasazi occupation. Changes in detail and design enable them to trace cultural development. In the late Developmental Pueblo Period, for example, the Anasazi began making corrugated pottery for

*T*he four-story "tower" area of Cliff Palace would have looked more like an apartment house when the Anasazi lived in the dwelling. Cliff Palace was built on various terraced levels, illustrating the architectural skills of these stone-age masons. Visitors marvel at the tall, straight walls with their precise corners.

kitchen use. On such pots the Anasazi pinched the surface with their fingers to give the clay a rough texture. Visitors can see the changes in the distinctive Mesa Verde black-on-white and corrugated pottery in exhibits at the Chapin Mesa Archeological Museum.

Neither Modified Basket Maker nor Developmental Pueblo Anasazi led an isolated existence. Even though they had to travel on foot, there is evidence of elaborate trade networks. Excavations reveal red pottery with black designs—a color the local clay would not produce. The Anasazi wove cotton textiles, yet the Mesa Verde climate is not conducive to the growth of cotton. It had to have been brought in through trade with people in northern Arizona.

Most turquoise found in Mesa Verde originally came from the Cerrillos Hills between Santa Fe and Albuquerque, New Mexico. Shell beads and bracelets came from as far as the Gulf of California. Undoubtedly, ideas were also exchanged. The Anasazi must have had as much curiosity about other people and their customs as we do today.

THE GREAT PUEBLO PERIOD

The years A.D. 1100 to 1300 mark what is called the Great Pueblo Period, the "golden age" of the Anasazi in the Mesa Verde area. There were no radical changes which inaugurated this period, but rather a refining of cultural elements arising out of the earlier periods. Probably the most notable cause for this cultural climax stems from perfecting their agricultural skills. Using improved varieties of corn, the Anasazi could increase their yields. They had already developed check dams in drainages where additional crops could be grown. By increasing the amount of arable land, the Anasazi could concentrate more time on projects involving arts and crafts, religion, and social organization.

During the Great Pueblo Period the Anasazi moved from small, scattered villages all over the mesa tops to larger, more compact communities. Often dwellings became multi-storied structures, as many as four stories high. Kivas, which had been located in the open away from house units, began to be incorporated within the walls of the village itself. Kiva roofs formed enclosed plazas where work could be concentrated. Stone towers, sometimes connected to a kiva by a tunnel, may have been built for lookout or signaling purposes or some symbolic religious belief. Towers located in prominent positions certainly afforded excellent views of the surrounding countryside.

In earlier times stones used in house construction were roughhewn and unevenly shaped. Some sites did contain wedge-shaped stones chipped fairly evenly, but Great Pueblo Period

▲ **Anasazi stonework varies from crude to truly elaborate.** Skilled craftsmen chipped and shaped the stones, giving some walls a smooth, finished texture, while others indicate shoddy workmanship—human nature at work!

builders increasingly made rectangular stones of a uniform size. They chipped and shaped the stones, pecking the surface to create a dimpled effect. These stones were pleasing to the eye—a craftsman's delight! They required less mortar to hold them together. Within the mortar the Anasazi placed little chinking stones to fill in gaps and alleviate cracking. Clearly, the architectural construction epitomized by Sun Temple was the hallmark of Mesa Verde builders.

In the late 1190s and early 1200s, the Anasazi began constructing the cliff dwellings for which Mesa Verde is famous. Why they built giants such as Cliff Palace and Long House, no one really knows. The sheltering alcoves provided relief from wind, rain, and snow, avoiding the effects of climate. They may have been defensive structures protecting them from other people, although there is limited evidence of warfare or invading peoples in the area. There may have been religious or emotional motives. At any rate, it appears the majority of people moved into the cliffs, though some stayed in mesa-top villages such as Far View.

Of the over 4,000 sites in Mesa Verde National Park, only about 600 are cliff dwellings. Most visitors arrive with the impression that all cliff dwellings are large units such as Spruce Tree House and Cliff Palace. However, the vast majority are small, containing fewer than 20 rooms each.

There is a high ratio of kivas to living rooms in the large sites, yet most of the small ones have no kivas at all. The dwellings face various directions, indicating that the Anasazi used whatever alcove was available. Some have water sources in them, while others required carrying water from nearby springs.

In front of or below cliff dwellings archaeologists find Anasazi refuse or trash heaps. Materials such as broken pottery, bone or stone tools, discarded yucca fiber sandals, worn-out clothing, cold ashes from fires, human waste, and a variety of corn cobs, squash, and other food were all thrown in these areas. Archaeological excavators sift through these trash heaps in an attempt to locate materials for reconstructing information about the daily lives of the Anasazi. These trash slopes enable them to answer many questions that would otherwise remain a mystery.

The Anasazi commonly buried their dead in these refuse areas. This practice had nothing to do with any dishonor or disrespect; the loose material was probably much easier to dig than the surrounding ground, especially during the winter months when it was frozen. The body was usually buried in a flexed position with the knees drawn up to the chest and wrapped in a yucca-fiber mat, rabbit-fur robe, or turkey-feather blanket.

Objects such as pottery and tools, which might be considered useful in the next life, were buried with the individual. Jewelry and ornaments were other typical possessions placed on the bodies. Because burials are found in a variety of places and many of them could have been disturbed or dug up by animals, archaeologists may never be able to account for the number which should be found in Mesa Verde.

The solitary winter visitor sees the alcoves framed in snow—a picture worth a thousand words. Those who take a morning tour of Spruce Tree House find out how cold and miserable the alcoves can be. It is easy to imagine the Anasazi huddled around fires, dressed in skins and hides, and using turkey-feather blankets to keep warm. It is equally easy to idealize these eminently talented people, yet theirs was a harsh life with many of the same pitfalls facing people today.

Abandonment Of Mesa Verde

Why did the Anasazi build such massive dwellings only to abandon them in less than 100 years? In the late 1200s there was a serious drought which must have taken a toll on harvests and productivity. Yet, the Anasazi had survived

◀ **H**ouse of Many Windows is typical of small cliff dwellings. Tucked into precarious alcoves not easily accessible, such dwellings are scattered up and down the canyons of Mesa Verde. This dwelling contained about 15 rooms, housing 15-20 people. The Anasazi scampered back and forth to the mesa top on a daily basis.

previous droughts. By the late 1200s good farmland may have been depleted. Timber resources and game animals may have been scarce. A cooling-off period, almost like a mini-ice age, could have shortened the growing season and prevented the Anasazi from continuing as successful farmers.

In addition, the peak of population occurred in the later years. Perhaps too many people competed for available natural resources. Information exchanged through trade contacts must have told them that dynamic communities to the south were flourishing. Maybe they were drawn to such places despite the ties to their ancestral homes.

For whatever reasons, the Anasazi migrated out of the area over a 25-50 year span. It was not a massive migration, but rather a slow movement southward. Probably some had dreams of returning to the land that had been so good to them. But fate has its way of determining history, and the Anasazi never returned. The former splendor of the cliff dwellings deteriorated with the ravages of time. Only the spirit of the Anasazi remained.

SUGGESTED READING

Jones, Dewitt, and Linda S. Cordell. *Anasazi World*. Portland, Oregon: Graphic Arts Center Publishing Co., 1985.

Lister, Robert H. and Florence C. *Mesa Verde National Park: Preserving the Past*. Santa Barbara, California: Sequoia Communications, 1987.

Wenger, Gilbert R. *The Story of Mesa Verde National Park*. Mesa Verde Museum Association, Inc., 1980.

▲ **M**esa-top sites such as Pipe Shrine House appear picturesque covered in snow. However, the winter visitor who trudges through the snow quickly learns how difficult it was for the Anasazi. Clay pipes excavated from one of the rooms gave the dwelling its name.

Cliff Palace

GEORGE H. H. HUEY

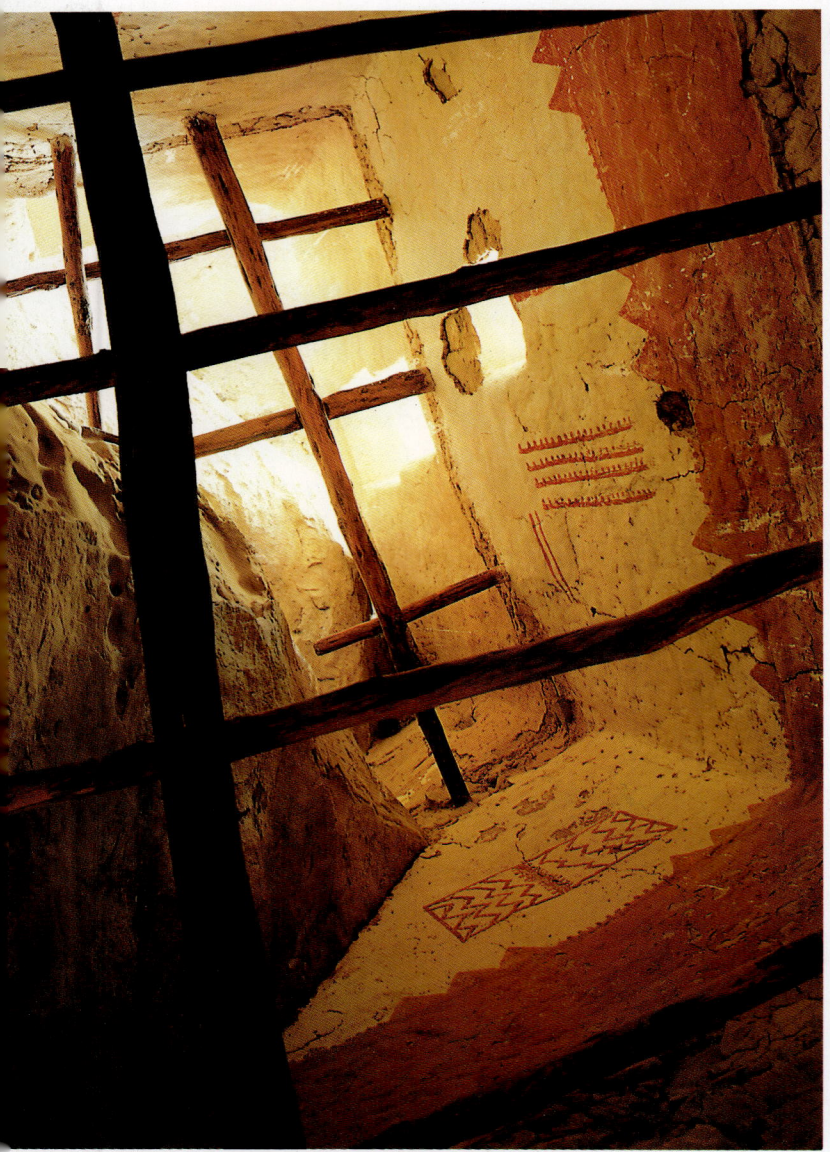

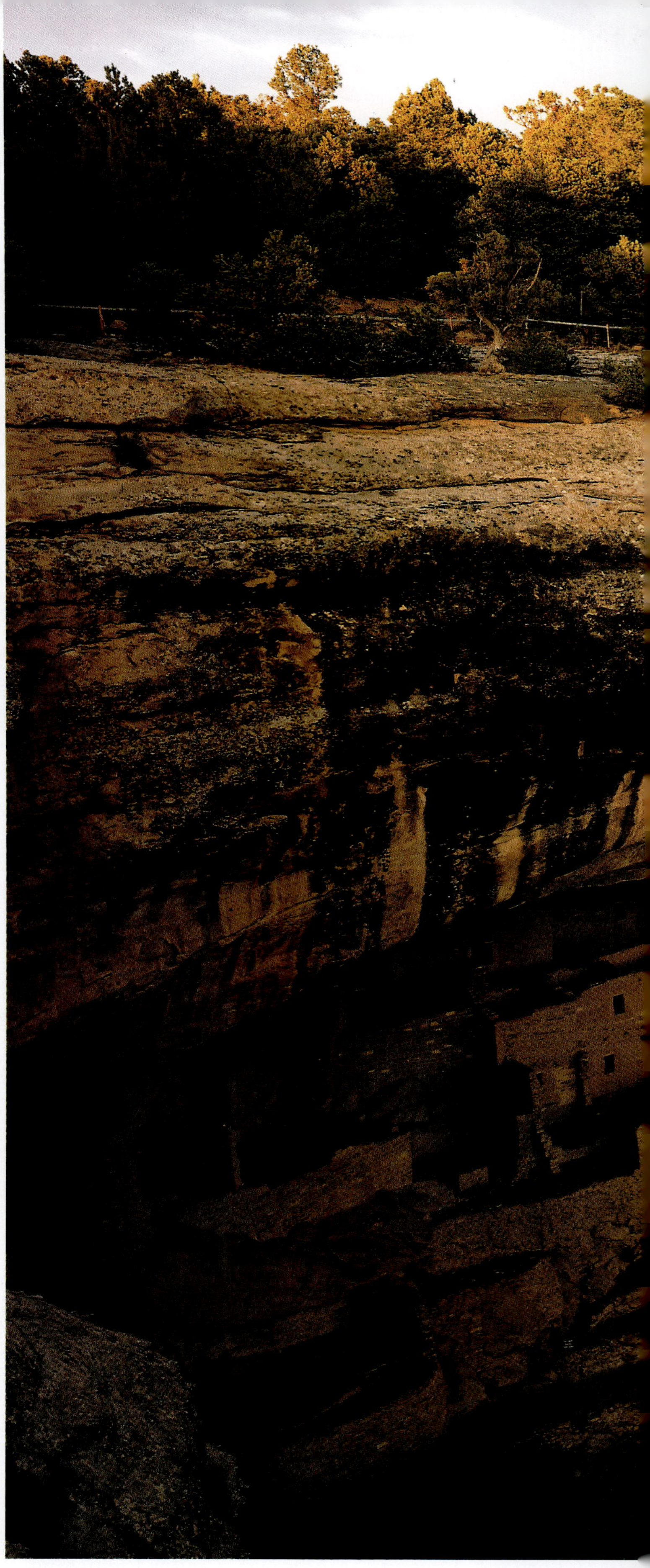

TOM DANIELSEN

This painting inside the four-story section of *Cliff Palace is remarkably well-preserved. Many Anasazi designs are geometric figures or patterns painted on a reddish-brown or off-white background. There is no written record to explain what they mean. Some of them may be symbolic or merely decoration in a living room. Regardless of their purpose, they are a tribute to the artistic talent of the Anasazi.*

▲ **What a thrill it must have been for the cowboys who discovered Cliff Palace on that winter day in 1888.** Nestled in a huge alcove, the dwelling contains 217 rooms and 23 kivas, housing around 250 people during the 1200s. Think about what a bustling community it was! Major stabilization has been done to front sections of the dwelling, but some of the finest walls remain intact. Rooms average 6 by 8 feet in size, with smaller rooms used mainly as storage areas.

Far View

TERRY DONNELLY

The Far View area consists of a series *of mesa-top dwellings occupied from the A.D. 900s until the abandonment of Mesa Verde. The double course masonry walls are composed of finely shaped stones held together by mud mortar. Lintels over doorways were either stone slabs or pieces of wood set into the surrounding sandstone blocks. Today these walls are heavily stabilized to withstand severe weather conditions and the wear and tear of thousands of yearly visitors who can roam freely over them. A few of the kivas are larger and deeper than those in cliff dwellings. What a chore it must have been to chop down enough trees to roof over so many kivas and rooms. No wonder the Anasazi used up a lot of their timber resources!*

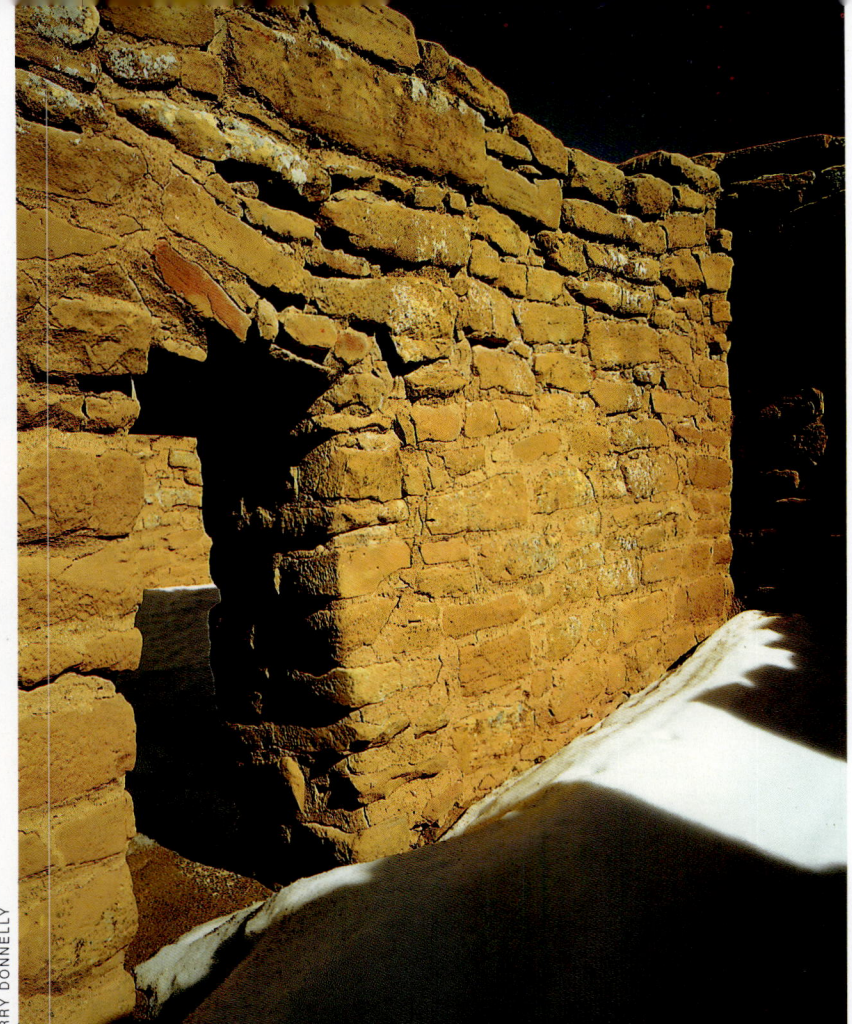

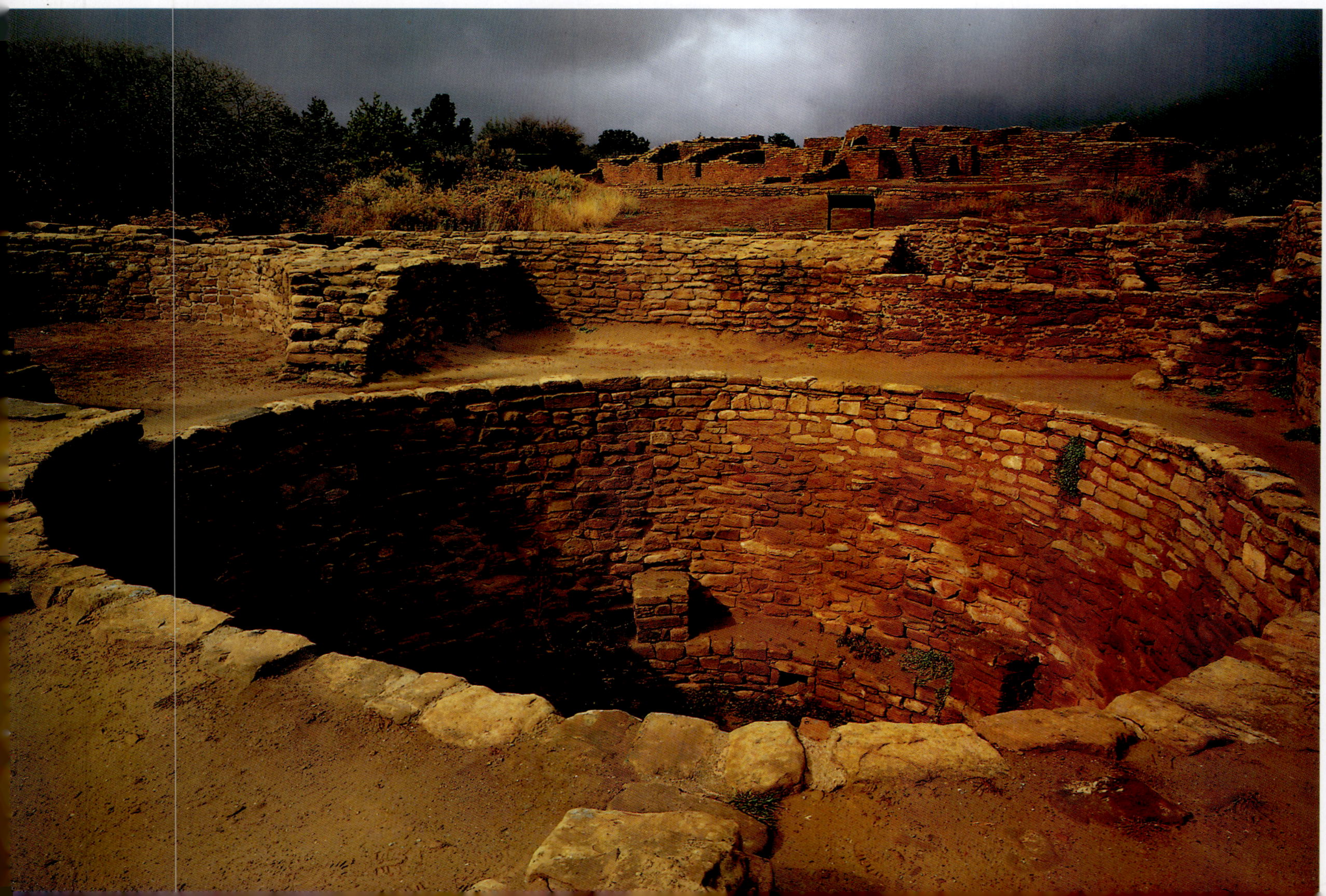

JOHN P. GEORGE

Sun Temple

▲ *Located on the mesa top across the canyon from Cliff Palace, Sun Temple was built in the 1200s and may never have been completed. There is no evidence that a roof covered the rooms or kivas. Few potsherds or other household artifacts were found during the excavation of this D-shaped dwelling by Jesse Walter Fewkes in 1915. Archaeologists believe it may have been a ceremonial structure for a large community. No other mesa-top dwelling is enclosed by double walls with long, narrow rooms between them. The stones making up the walls are shaped by pecking. Fewkes put a concrete capping on the walls to prevent deterioration from rain and snow. Without the capping water would penetrate into the core, eroding the mud mortar in the walls. The capping also serves as a walkway for visitors.*

▲ **Spruce Tree House, the third-largest cliff dwelling** in the park, contains 114 rooms and 8 kivas. Visitors notice extensive smoke blackening on the roof of the alcove and wonder what it was like for the 125-150 occupants who inhaled so much smoke. No doubt the Anasazi were thrilled to see the first signs of spring return each year.

With its location directly behind the Chapin Mesa Museum, Spruce Tree House is often the first cliff dwelling visitors see. It is also the only dwelling open on a year-round basis. The spring at the head of the box canyon provided a good water supply for its inhabitants. ▼

Square Tower

Like Cliff Palace, Square Tower House contains a four-story ▷ *unit which functioned like an apartment complex with rooms radiating to the side. There are about 80 rooms and 7 kivas in this large dwelling. Two of the kivas have portions of original roofs remaining. They were used as examples for the reconstructed kiva roofs in Spruce Tree House. The dry southwest climate allowed wood to survive many centuries of natural weathering intact.*

RUSS FINLEY

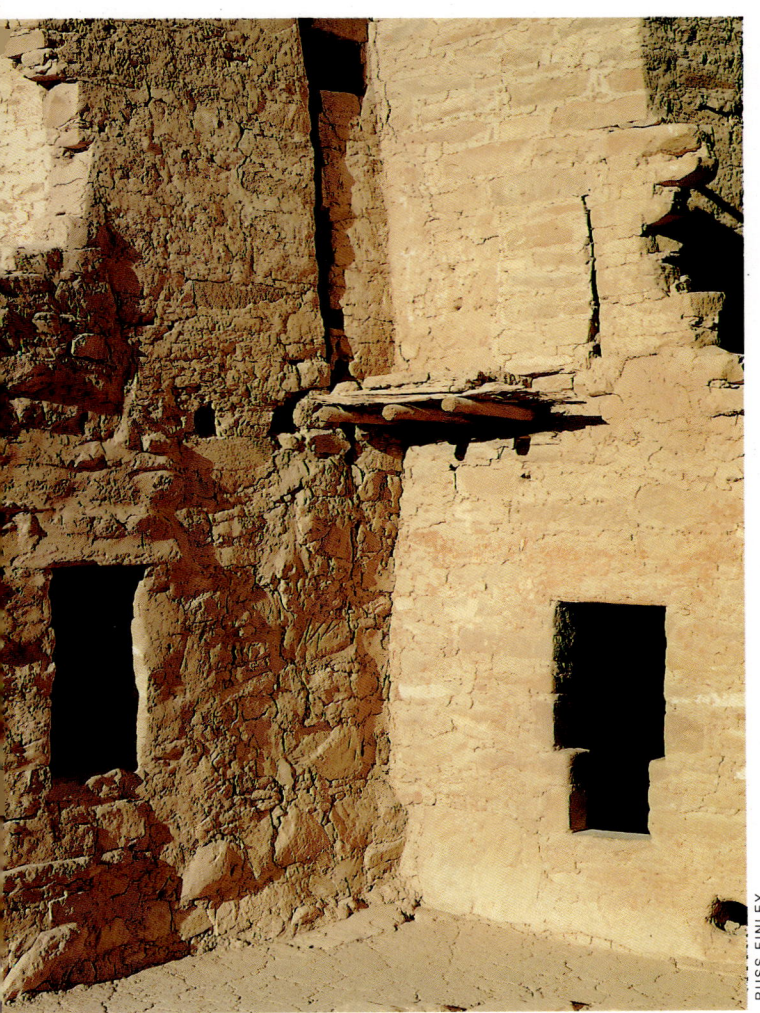

△ **A segment of a balcony juts out from a Spruce** *Tree House wall. At one time the balcony extended across about a 20-foot span. Ladders leading up to such balconies served as access to second-story rooms.*

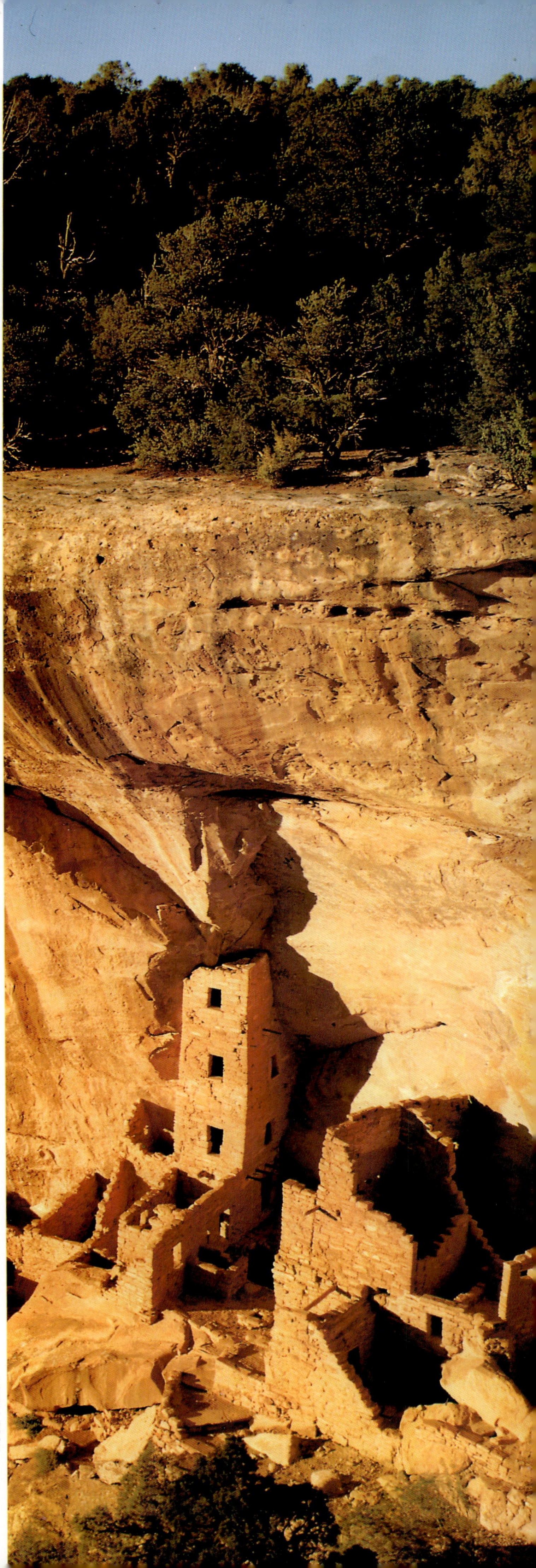

RUSS FINLEY

Fire Temple

Fire Temple in Fewkes ▷
Canyon is one of only two dance plaza areas in Mesa Verde. In the center of the plaza is the firepit, surrounded by two troughs which may have been foot drums for the Anasazi. When ceremonies were in progress, chanting voices probably resonated throughout the canyon.

ELIOT COHEN

New Fire House

New Fire House, located adjacent to Fire Temple in Fewkes Canyon, contains 20 rooms and 3 kivas. It is unusual for a dwelling so small to have that many kivas. A close look at the alcove shows toeholds carved into the cliff leading to the upper level. Upper ledges often seem inaccessible today, but the Anasazi built rooms two and three stories high reaching to upper levels. Otherwise, ladders or toeholds served as access.

Most cliff dwellings are small, single family units rather than the large ones open to the public. Typically composed of five or six rooms, a small dwelling might have a couple of storage rooms, two or three sleeping rooms, and at least one room with a firepit for cooking. The majority of these small dwellings have no kivas. Probably people living in small alcoves went to larger ones to participate in ceremonial or religious activities. Most of these small sites also remain unexcavated. They receive periodic stabilization and are being preserved for future research purposes.

The Anasazi must have visited their neighbors in nearby canyons on a regular basis. Scrambling up and down trails was an everyday occurrence. In the process they could gather wild plants, bring water from springs, gossip with other people, and exchange pottery, jewelry, or other items they made. There must have been a sense of community even for the most isolated people.

GAIL BANDINI

A tour of Balcony ▷ House is an adventure. Visitors climb a 32-foot ladder to enter the dwelling and crawl through a 12-foot tunnel to exit. There are only 35-40 rooms and 2 kivas, but the experience leaves a lasting impression.

Cedar Tree Tower is an example of how the Anasazi often linked a tower to a kiva. Perhaps the tunnel to the kiva allowed them to signal people inside of approaching danger. Archaeologists are uncertain if there was a threat or an entirely different reason for the connection. ▽

Cedar Tree Tower

Balcony House

▲ **A**lthough originally called Brownstone Front, the present name, Balcony House, seems more appropriate. The balcony in the first courtyard is beautifully preserved. From it the Anasazi could work, have a view of Soda Canyon, and watch their children all at the same time.

▲ **E**verything about Balcony House was precarious for the Anasazi. When the kivas were roofed, you could walk right off the edge of the cliff. It looks more defensive than other dwellings, yet archaeologists have no idea what the problems were.

◀ **E**xamining the mortar between sandstone blocks reveals small chinking stones inserted into the mud. They are prominent in much original cliff-dwelling construction, and stabilization crews duplicate the effect when repairs are necessary. As a finishing touch, the Anasazi put a coating of plaster over the stones and mortar.

Overleaf: *Square Tower House* ▶
*offers one of the most picturesque settings in Mesa Verde.
Photo by John P. George.*

*The Ute people knew about
the existence of houses in the cliffs,
but did not go there because
"when the spirits of the dead are disturbed,
then you die too."*

Historic Mesa Verde

If Mesa Verde has a fascinating prehistoric chronology, it has an equally intriguing historic one. Exactly how soon other people entered the area after the Anasazi left is a good question. The earliest evidence of the Utes, Navajos, or Apaches arriving is in the later 1400s. Yet, none of these groups moved onto the mesa tops or into the alcoves. The Ute people knew about the existence of houses in the cliffs, but did not go there because "when the spirits of the dead are disturbed, then you die too." Cultural tradition played a definite role in how they viewed the "ancient ones."

EARLY EXPLORATION PERIOD

Spanish accounts record a party passing through the Mesa Verde region in 1765. Then in 1776, the famous Dominguez-Escalante expedition explored north of the park, camping for a while near Dolores, Colorado. Somewhere along the line the Spanish named the area, for Mesa Verde is a Spanish term meaning "green table." Today, visitors coming into the park look up and see the fairly flat, lush, green tableland.

For the next 100 years Mesa Verde remained essentially an unknown entity. Isolated references

▲ **The north escarpment was the view of Mesa Verde seen by Spanish exploring parties and other travelers.** Its rugged slopes and forbidding appearance may have steered them onward to other areas. They had no idea what spectacular ruins lay hidden in the canyons to the south. Even today many visitors do not realize that it is a winding 20-mile drive from the entrance of the park to their first sight of a cliff dwelling.

◀ **Spruce Tree House may have been framed in** snow when the Wetherills discovered it. They climbed down a Douglas fir tree growing in front of the dwelling to enter the alcove. At that time a Douglas fir was considered to be a spruce, giving the dwelling its name.

to dwellings do appear, and some explorers even wandered into a few canyons. However, it was not until 1874 that pioneer photographer William Henry Jackson entered Mancos Canyon, where he photographed Two Story House. Although this dwelling is outside park boundaries, this was the first photograph of a cliff dwelling in the vicinity. The silence which had engulfed the abandoned alcoves was broken forever.

DISCOVERY OF THE CLIFF DWELLINGS

In 1880, a restless Benjamin Wetherill moved his wife and family to Mancos, Colorado, to establish the Alamo cattle ranch. His five sons and one daughter worked hard to make their father's ranch successful. They befriended the local Ute people, and during the winter months grazed their cattle in Mancos Canyon. The Wetherills heard about houses in the cliffs from Ute friends. In their spare time the cowboys journeyed up the canyons looking for stray cattle and anything else of interest. On a fateful day in December 1888, Richard Wetherill and his brother-in-law, Charlie Mason, discovered Cliff Palace. Before leaving, they also located Spruce Tree House and Square Tower House. They were so excited that they rushed home to tell the rest of the family about their thrilling discovery.

◀ **When Gustaf** Nordenskiold searched for relics in Mesa Verde in 1891, he stored his camera equipment in a dwelling on what he called Wetherill Mesa. This dwelling, Kodak House, remains unexcavated and is only viewed from an overlook. It contains 70 or more rooms built on two levels and faces Rock Canyon to the west. One wonders whether Nordenskiold realized how important his photography would be in documenting a site and publicizing the area.

Soon the Wetherills busied themselves taking collections out of the cliff dwellings and guiding tourists into the ruins. The Alamo Ranch became a prominent tourist destination. Benjamin Wetherill realized that this discovery could be one of great importance. He wrote to the Smithsonian Institution to see if they would like to buy an artifact collection, and asked for guidance in exploring the ruins. Unfortunately, since the Smithsonian was short on funds, it passed up the opportunity. Meanwhile, the Wetherills packed up artifacts for promotional purposes, displaying them in cities across the country.

News spread about the cliff dwellings. In June 1891, a Swedish tourist named Gustaf Nordenskiold decided that he wanted to see them personally. He had a scientific background and was enthralled by the ancient relics. He not only did the first scientific excavation work in the dwellings, he also wrote one of the first books about the area, *The Cliff Dwellers of the Mesa Verde*. Nordenskiold created local resentment by shipping a collection of the discovered artifacts back to Sweden when he left Colorado. His legacy remains in the photographs he took and the research he conducted.

THE CREATION OF A PARK

A "New York Graphic" correspondent, Virginia Donaghe McClurg, visited Mesa Verde in 1892. She became almost a one-woman bandwagon to preserve the cliff dwellings and create a park out of them. Intensive lobbying began when her promotional efforts stimulated the endorsement of the Colorado Federation of Women's Clubs. By 1900, she incorporated the Colorado Cliff Dwellings Association with herself as regent. Lucy Peabody, a savvy Washington socialite, also took up the cause. Since the cliff dwellings were on Ute Reservation land, these women worked with the Utes toward a land agreement.

Victorian women were not in the vanguard of national politics, but through their efforts Congress passed and President Theodore Roosevelt signed a bill creating Mesa Verde National Park on June 29, 1906.

PRESERVATION TAKES PRECEDENCE

Even though there was no adequate road into the park, cliff-dwelling preservation took precedence in the first few years. Jesse Walter Fewkes, working for the Smithsonian Institution, excavated 16 different sites in Mesa Verde, starting with Spruce Tree House in 1908. During the summer of 1909, Fewkes excavated and stabilized Cliff Palace. Later he worked at Far View and Sun Temple. In the course of this work, Fewkes also gave the first campfire programs in the National Park Service.

Probably the most influential figure in Mesa Verde National Park's history was Jesse Nusbaum. He originally came to the park in 1907 to survey and photograph ruins. In 1910, he excavated and stabilized Balcony House. From 1921 to 1931, as superintendent, he transformed a struggling operation into an effectively administered park. It was Nusbaum's design which became the architectural style for the Chapin Mesa Museum and other headquarters buildings. He even established the first interpretive programs such as conducting guided tours of the ruins.

This view of Cliff Canyon is taken from near Sun Temple where Fewkes Canyon enters into Cliff Canyon. In this vicinity is the largest concentration of cliff dwellings anywhere in the park. What an incredible assortment of ruins caught the cowboys' eyes when they first arrived. Fewkes excavated many of the sites during the years 1915-1920, and the small canyon bears his name.

▲ **The highlight of the Chapin Mesa Museum for many visitors is seeing the five dioramas depicting time periods** in Mesa Verde prehistory. Each diorama concentrates on a separate aspect of architectural achievement. The Spruce Tree House diorama chronicles the Classic Pueblo Period from A.D. 1100 to 1300.

Visitors are especially interested in the history of the dioramas—how they were made and who was involved in their creation. Each figure is so meticulously crafted it appears they were made by machine, but this was not the case. They were constructed from the mid-1930s to the early 1940s, mostly by park employees with the help of crew members from the Civilian Conservation Corps (CCC) camps that were in the park at that time. (This project was only one of many in the park that involved the CCC.)

▲ **This building houses the National Park Service** administrative offices. It is one of several buildings in the historic district built in the 1920s and early 1930s. Each building was architecturally designed to blend in with the cliff-dwelling motif.

In 1913, the first wagons drove all the way from Mancos to Spruce Tree House, and by 1914 the first cars traveled this new road. This was a major breakthrough in encouraging more visitors to enter the park. There are still tales about one section of the road called the "Knife Edge." It was so steep and precarious that it was finally abandoned in 1957, when a tunnel was constructed as a shorter and safer route to Chapin Mesa.

No visitor can leave Mesa Verde without seeing examples of work done by the Civilian Conservation Corps. Several CCC camps were set up in the park in 1934. Enrollees built everything from a water system to trails to the Chapin Mesa Museum dioramas. Without their labor the park would not be what it is today.

An Ambitious Scientific Investigation

From 1958 to 1963, the National Park Service, in conjunction with the National Geography Society, inaugurated the most ambitious scientific investigation of Mesa Verde to date. This was the Wetherill Mesa Archaeological Project, an attempt to survey, excavate, and stabilize mesa-top and cliff-dwelling sites as well as conduct other laboratory research. Long House and Step House

In 1957, Park Service employees constructed a ▲ tunnel from Morefield Canyon to Prater Canyon, thereby effectively bypassing a section of the entrance road considered too treacherous to maintain.

were opened to the public as a result of this project. Archaeological investigation alone cost more than $1 million—an incredible amount of money for that time period!

These are only a few of the significant events in the history of Mesa Verde. Archaeological research continues, and stabilization efforts to keep sites in good repair are ongoing projects. To this day, Mesa Verde is the only national park set aside to protect the works of people—a tribute to its creators.

SUGGESTED READING

SMITH, DUANE A. *Mesa Verde National Park: Shadows of the Centuries.* Lawrence, Kansas: University Press of Kansas, 1988.

SMITH, JACK E. *Mesas, Cliffs, and Canyons.* Mesa Verde Museum Association, Inc., 1987.

Long House

▲ **Long** House, the ▷ second-largest cliff dwelling in Mesa Verde, was excavated as part of the Wetherill Mesa Archeological Project from 1958-1963. The long alcove provides one of the most active springs in the park. Moisture-laden moss still coats the back area, where visitors can see hollowed-out potholes used for water collection. The 150-175 residents built around 150 rooms and 21 kivas in the alcove. They also constructed a great kiva or dance plaza similar to Fire Temple on Chapin Mesa. Because the dwelling has a southern exposure, it receives ample sunlight during winter months. All of these advantages must have been important to the Anasazi who lived here.

Step House

▲ **Step House on Wetherill Mesa is significant because it is one of the few** cliff dwellings where visitors can see both Basket Maker and Pueblo occupations. A prehistoric staircase leading to the mesa top gives the dwelling its name. Jesse Nusbaum partially excavated the site in 1926, and the remainder was excavated as part of the Wetherill Mesa Project.

JACK OLSON

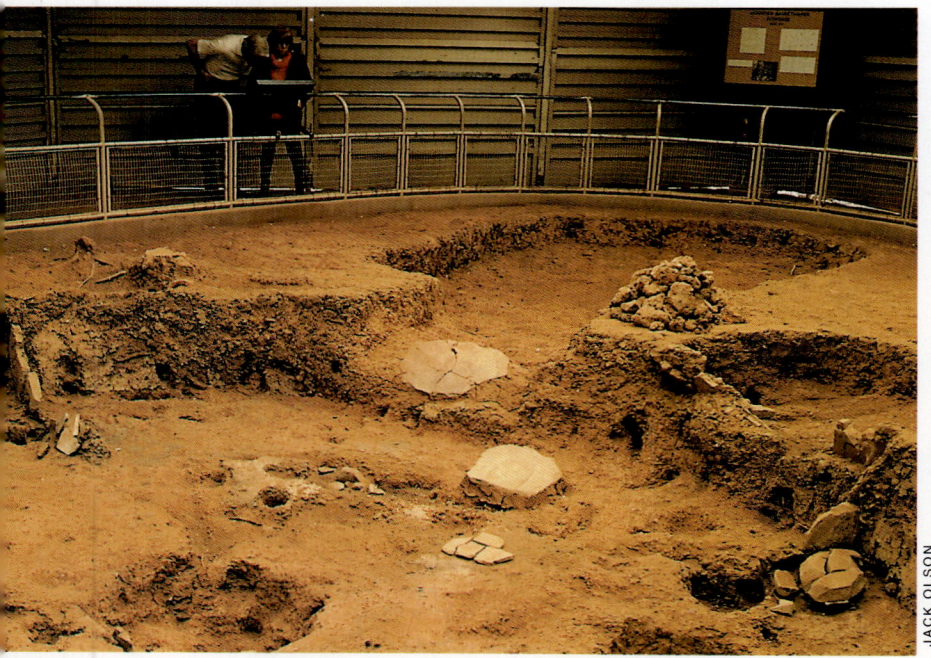

Pithouse B represents the earliest period of *construction in the park dating to A.D. 575. It was excavated by James A. Lancaster in 1941, in an attempt to chronicle the cultural sequence on the mesa top. Like many other pit houses, the roof had burned, but most of the other features were intact. Original plaster is visible, and the mud floor remains in good condition.*

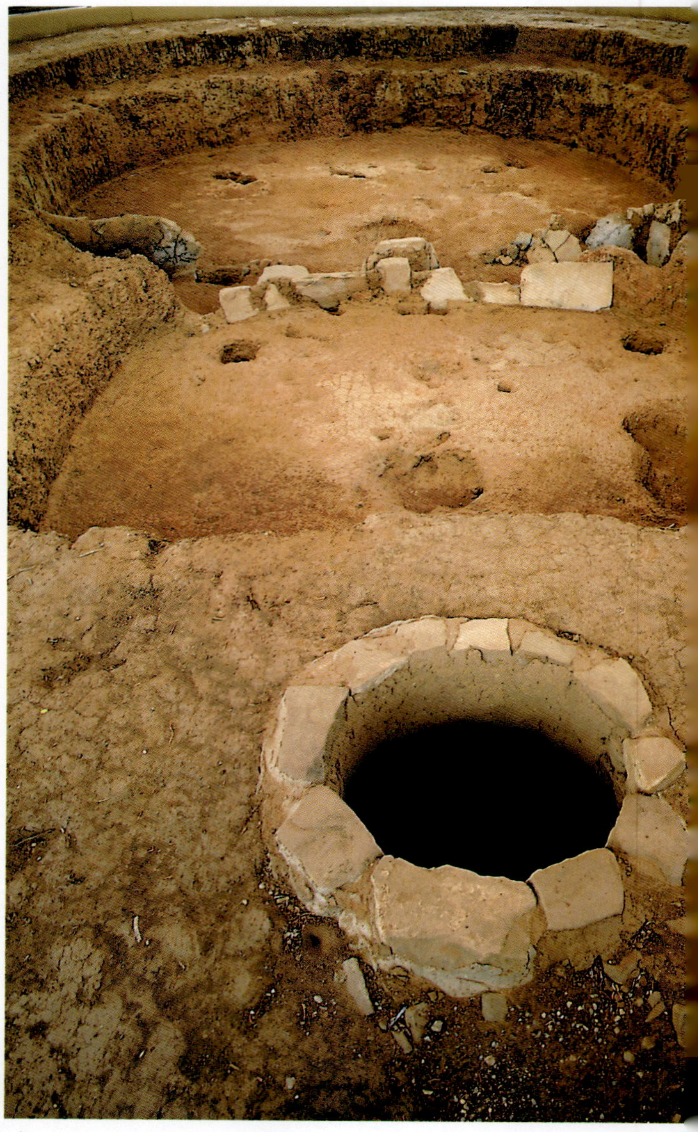

TOM DANIELSON

There are actually two pit houses shown *here. The smaller one in front overlaps the earlier one dated A.D. 674. It was characteristic of Mesa Verde pit houses to be dug deeper in the later years—notice how much deeper these are than Pithouse B. You can easily distinguish the two firepits and the postholes that were for logs supporting the roofs.*

THOMAS L. MAXWELL

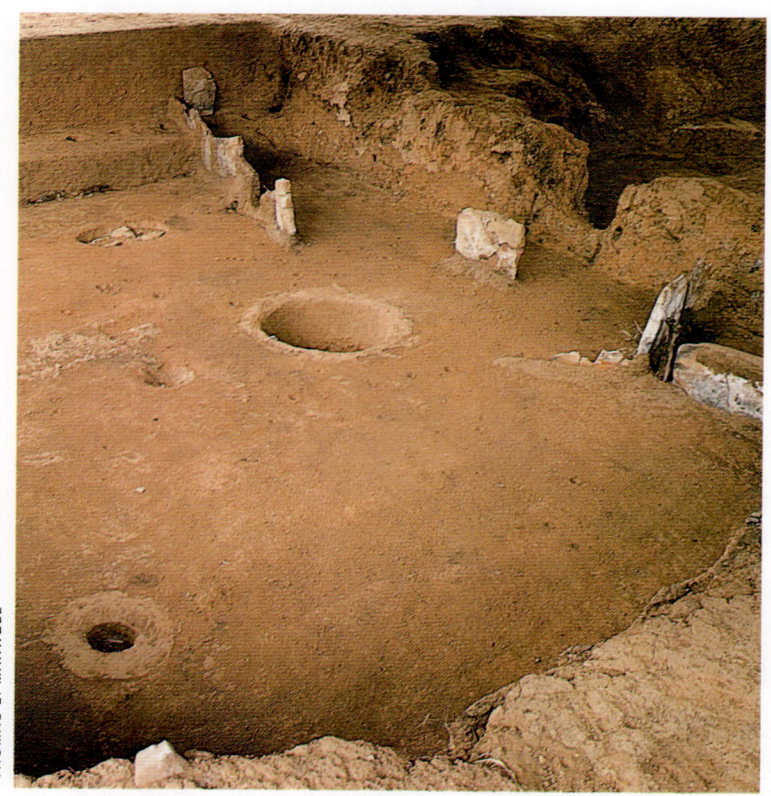

Access to most pit houses was through *an opening in the roof or via an antechamber—a small room connected to the pit house itself. In this example the stone slabs jutting out from either side of the firepit are called wing walls and help delineate the cooking area.*

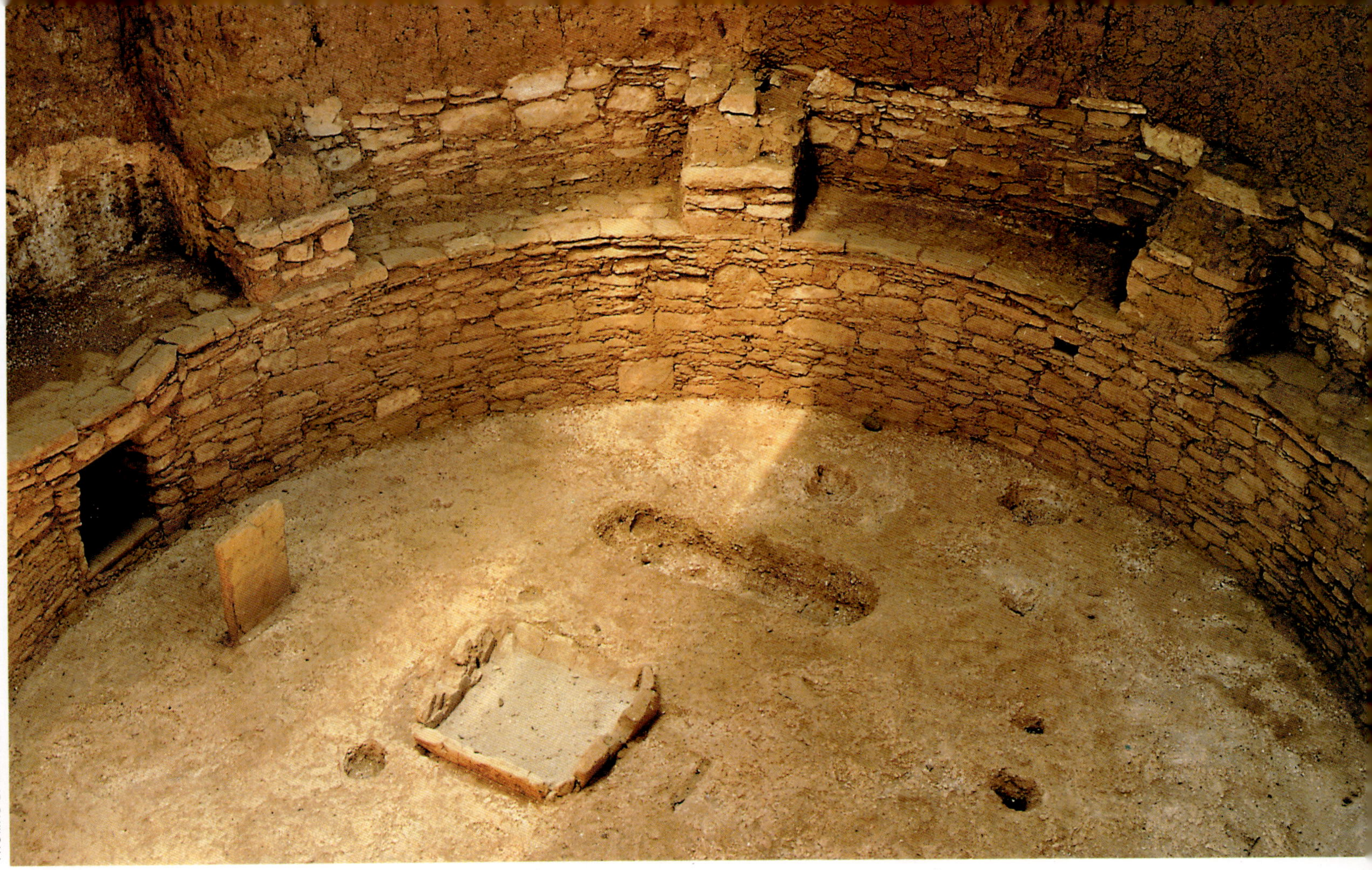

THOMAS L. MAXWELL

This kiva, built around A.D. 1075, is associated with one of the villages at Site 16 on the Mesa Top loop. It is *larger in diameter than many, and contains eight pilasters, or roof supports, rather than the usual six. Most kivas had a good ventilation system. When a fire was built, fresh air was drawn down the ventilator shaft (the hole in the side wall) circling around the kiva, and smoke rose through the central opening in the roof.*

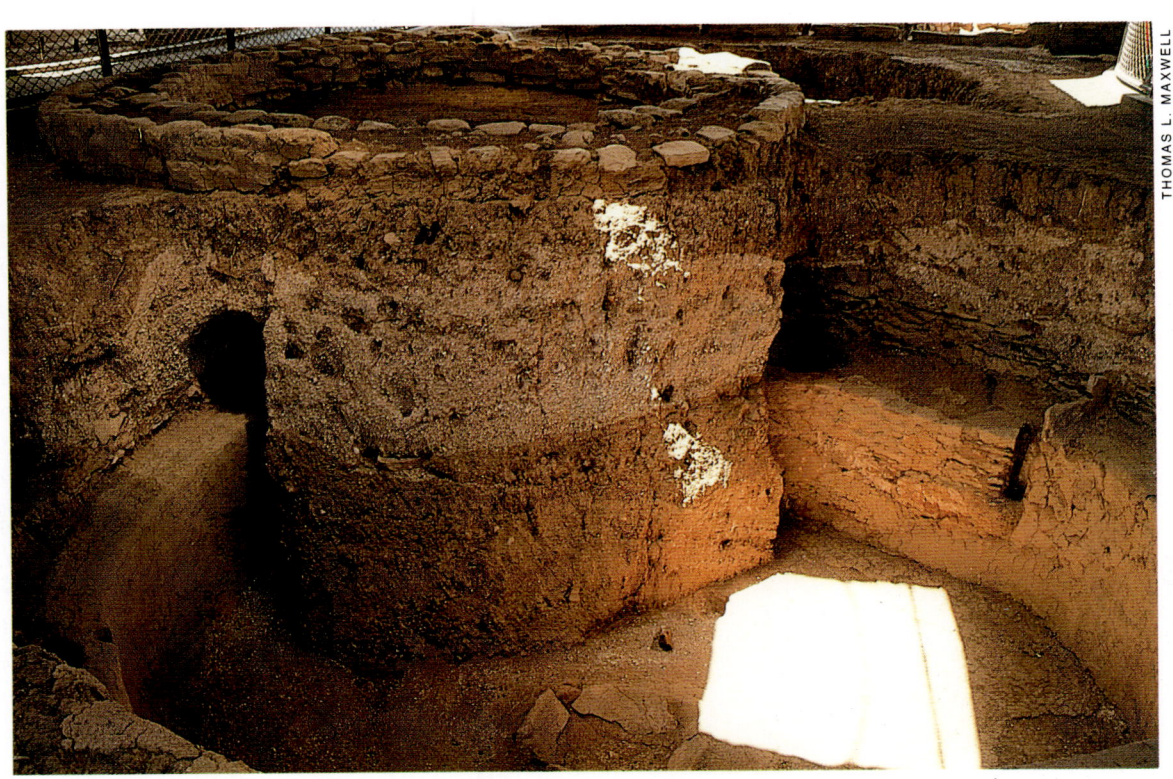

The kiva shown *here was an earlier structure than the ring of stones at ground level. These stones are the base of a tower built over the earlier site, a common occurrence in Developmental Pueblo architecture (A.D. 900 to 1100).*

THOMAS L. MAXWELL

▲ **Most Mesa Verde canyons** were formed by water erosion millions of years ago. The canyons are like fingers running north/south toward the Mancos River. Cliff Canyon is typical of side canyons where cliff dwellings are found in the upper band of sandstone. Lush vegetation in the canyon bottom makes walking difficult but is good browse for animals inhabiting the area. Access to the mesa top can be precarious, but the Anasazi knew exactly how to take advantage of this canyon environment.

◄ **It is not uncommon** for shale slopes to slump onto the entrance road of Mesa Verde, especially during spring freezing and thawing activity. The slump pictured here closed the park for an entire month in 1979 before major reinforcement made the road safe to travel again.

Geologic Forces

From Montezuma Valley ▷ overlook visitors get a panoramic view of where the notorious Knife Edge Road used to be. This road edged along the cliff face where all sorts of problems happened when the shale began to slide. At unexpected moments sandstone boulders came tumbling down on the road. If visitors are afraid of the road today—it's not the nightmare it once was!

◁ **Approaching the** park entrance the first glimpse people have is of Point Lookout, the sandstone-capped shale promontory looming over the valley. Actually, the elevation at the entrance (about 6,900 feet) is the same as it is at the cliff dwellings. You rise to 8,500 feet at Park Point and then drop to 7,000 feet again.

The lucky visitor who arrives in May or June when wildflowers are prolific sees splashes of red, blue, yellow, and white scattered across the mesa as it seems to come alive with these floral displays.

Nature's Prolific Preserve

Climatically, Mesa Verde is a semi-arid region with an average rainfall of about 18 inches—just sufficient for dryland farming. Summer temperatures rise to the mid-90s (Fahrenheit), while in winter the thermometer rarely drops much below zero. With a frost-free growing season of around 150 days, and mesa-top elevations ranging from 7,000 to 8,000 feet, Mesa Verde provides good habitat for farmers as well as special niches for diverse plants and animals.

Habitat Communities

The higher northern section of the park is covered by the mountain shrub community. Here Gambel oak, serviceberry, mountain mahogany, and cliff fendlerbush are interspersed with varieties of grasses. Some botanists believe these shrubs are abundant where forest fires have destroyed the tree cover. Others say they grow where unfavorable conditions, such as disease, have eliminated the trees.

◀ ***Navajo Canyon is*** one of the major drainages in the park, going all the way from Far View to the Mancos River. Cliff dwellings line the canyon walls, and from mesa top to canyon bottom is often 800 feet.

Biologists estimate that as many as 1,500 mule deer graze in the park. Their favorite food is the antelope bitterbrush which is plentiful in the headquarters area. During harsh winter months the deer move to lower elevations in surrounding valleys.

Along the north escarpment and in sheltered side canyons like the one where Spruce Tree House is located, stands of Douglas fir are prominent. Pinyon juniper forests cover the mesa tops and canyon slopes. The Anasazi used both varieties for construction materials and firewood.

From overlooks on Ruins Road, visitors see the deep canyon bottoms where there is a conspicuous absence of trees. Their gray-green color indicates dense growth of vegetation, including sagebrush, greasewood, saltbush, tomatillo, and prickly-pear cactus.

Flora and Fauna

The lucky visitor who arrives in May or June when wildflowers are prolific sees splashes of red, blue, yellow, and white scattered across the mesa as it seems to come alive with these floral displays.

Although the Mesa Verde vegetation is home to a wide variety of animals, mule deer are the most common. They browse so consistently in Morefield Campground and the Far View Lodge areas that nearly every visitor gets a close look at them. There is a small resident herd of elk, and an occasional black bear delights an observant visitor. Less frequently seen large mammals are the gray fox, badger, bobcat, and bighorn sheep.

Any park visitor who arrives from late August to early October sees a canopy of golden-blooming rabbitbrush along the road.

◀ **During the summer months both broad-tailed and** black-chinned hummingbirds breed in the park, using the same nests year after year.

▲ **Year-round residents like the Steller's jay** raucously scold anyone who disturbs them in picnic areas or along trails to the cliff dwellings.

Resident Birds and Other Critters

The most commonly seen birds are lustrous black ravens, raucously calling to one another or soaring overhead. Other year-round residents include scrub and Steller's jays, plain titmice, mountain chickadees, white-breasted nuthatches, and golden eagles. In 1990, the park reintroduced wild turkeys which have flourished in the Morefield and Prater Canyon areas. The truly dedicated bird watcher might even spy a peregrine falcon along the cliffs of the north escarpment.

Most visitors won't see any snakes during their visit to the park. In late summer and early fall, visitors report tarantulas crossing the road or along a trail. While they may appear ferocious, they are really very docile creatures.

Archaeological excavation reveals that present-day animal and plant species are the same as those living in Mesa Verde in prehistoric times. Refuse mounds contain an abundance of animal and bird bones, some of which were fashioned into tools. Pollen analysis clearly indicates what plants were cultivated or harvested. The diversity of flora and fauna in the park is amazing. No wonder the Anasazi lived for so long in what appears to be such a marginal environment!

SUGGESTED READING

ELMORE, FRANCIS H. *Shrubs and Trees of the Southwest Uplands.* Globe, Arizona: Southwest Parks and Monuments Association, 1976.

WENGER, STEPHEN R. *Flowers of Mesa Verde National Park.* Mesa Verde Museum Association, Inc., 1976.

▲ **Around sunset in the Spruce Tree House vicinity** 50-100 turkey vultures soar overhead, coming to rest in Douglas fir trees for the night.

▲ **Visitors regularly spot golden-mantled ground** squirrels filling their pouches in Morefield Campground. In cliff-dwelling areas chipmunks scurrying from place to place are more prominent, but both critters are a delight for children to watch.

▲ **Coyotes are a familiar sight sauntering along** roadways hunting for mice and rabbits. They dash into the pinyon/juniper forest at the sight of a car, only to reemerge and continue their search after the car passes.

▲ **Visitors occasionally see a bull snake** as they walk the path to one of the cliff dwellings. These non-poisonous snakes are hunting for mice and other critters, but they do not like being disturbed. They will sometimes coil like a rattlesnake and hiss to scare people away.

▲ **Beautiful turquoise and gold collared lizards often pose for** photographic enthusiasts going on tours. The larger, more colorful male stands out prominently compared to the female.

Useful Plants

▲ **The pinyon pine and Utah juniper forest prospers throughout most of the park. These hardy trees are drought** resistant, thriving where moisture is minimal. Every few years pinyons produce a crop of edible nuts highly prized for their flavor and caloric value—about 5,000 per pound! Native Americans eagerly gather the nuts, but they have to beat small animals and birds to them. Pinyon pitch, the resinous gum, was used to waterproof baskets. The bluish-gray juniper berries make tangy flavoring, but they have a biting, pungent taste taken directly from the trees. The shaggy juniper bark makes excellent bedding and was probably used for diapers by the Anasazi.

◀ **The leafless, joint-stemmed** Mormon tea is a cousin of the pinyon pine and juniper. A medicinal tea is made from the plant. Native Americans roast the seeds, eat them whole, or grind them into a meal.

▶ **G**rowing park-wide, broad-leaved yucca was one of the most useful plants for the Anasazi. Fibers produced cordage, sandals, leggings, and aprons. The cream-colored flowers made tasty salad or pot herbs. The banana-like fruits were eaten raw or cooked and dried as cakes.

△ **S**howy prickly-pear flowers bloom in June, later producing edible fruit that is sweet and gelatinous. Prickly-pear pads can be eaten raw after the spines are removed by rubbing or roasting. Scientific analysis showed that the Anasazi ate the pads despite the bristles.

▶ **S**ome prehistoric sites are covered with big sagebrush, telling archaeologists where to excavate. These gray-green shrubs commonly grow in deep canyon bottoms or on the mesa tops. They were boiled with alum to produce a green dye, and a tea from the leaves was an emetic.

*What a marvelous feeling to stand
at Park Point and look off for miles
in every direction with the same perspective
as the Anasazi had hundreds of years ago.*

Lessons for the Future

Because of its significance as a cultural preserve, Mesa Verde National Park, in 1978, was one of the first areas designated as a World Heritage Site. This distinction has since been shared by many National Park Service areas, but few places are so intensively visited by Europeans or other international groups.

Mesa Verde is a unique area set aside to protect over 4,000 archaeological sites. By guarding these cultural contributions, we are also preserving endangered plant species, threatened wildlife, and panoramic views of the American Southwest. What a marvelous feeling to stand at Park Point and look off for miles in every direction with the same perspective as the Anasazi had hundreds of years ago.

Preserving Priceless Artifacts

Given society's emphasis on material wealth, priceless artifacts such as pottery and basketry are threatened by the artifact hunter who is only

◀ **Artistically designed Mesa Verde black-on-white pottery** was shaped into mugs, bowls, ladles, and canteens. Its beauty is as admired today as it must have been in the thirteenth century.

▽ **Cliff Palace framed by snow on a sunny winter afternoon is a photographer's delight.**

MESA VERDE NATIONAL PARK

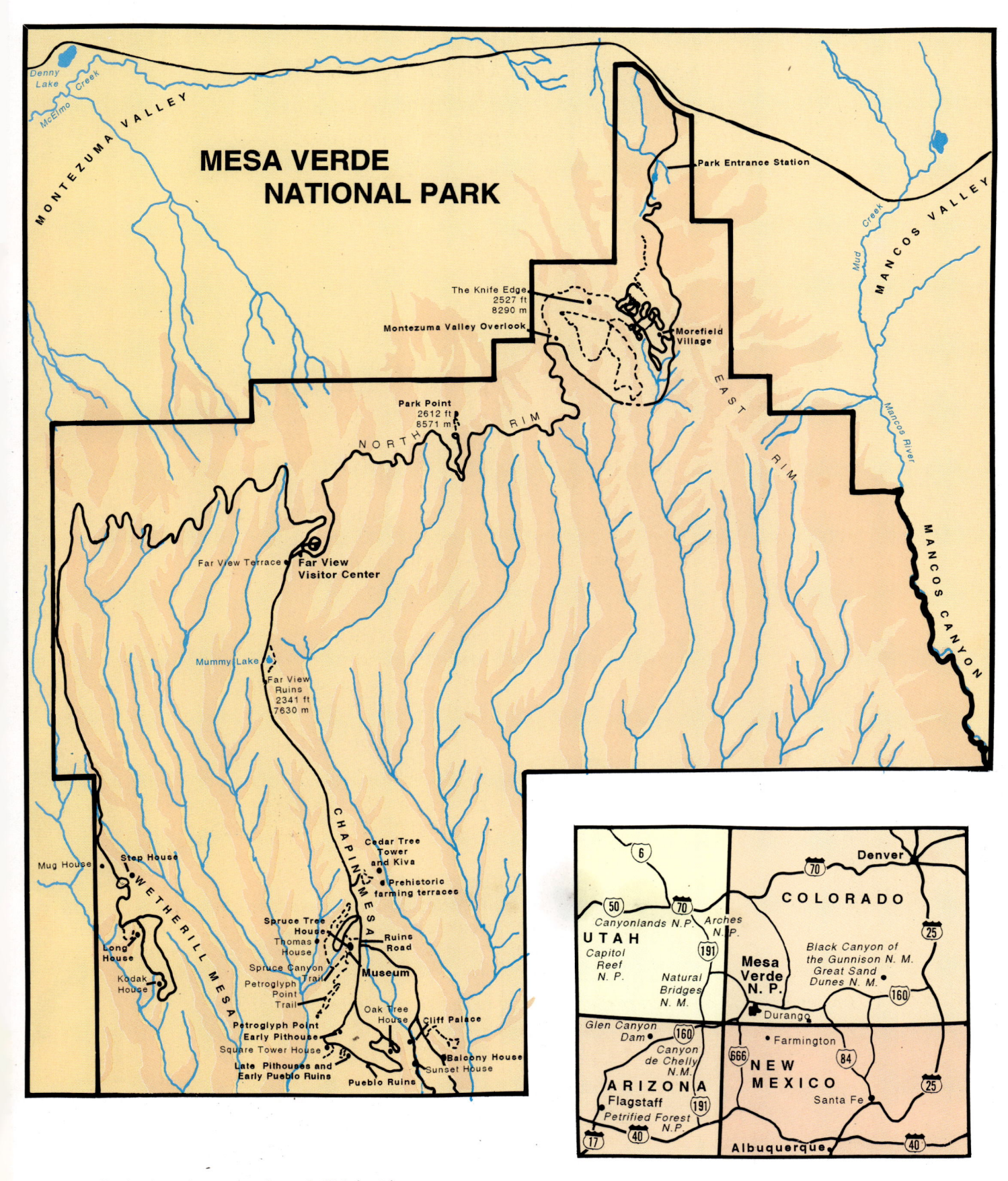

Park elevations vary from 6,200 feet in canyon bottoms to 8,500 feet at Park Point. Temperatures drop to zero degrees Fahrenheit in winter and rise to the mid-90s in summer.

Mesa Verde National Park has a unique status as the only cultural park in the system. It is also one of the few places where modern technology may never conquer its human drama. As scientists we can explain the architectural designs, the farming methods, the trade networks, or the pottery-making techniques. As historians we can document the overall pieces of human history. As human beings, however, we can never know for sure what the hopes and needs, wants and desires of the Anasazi were. Above all, they were people with some of the same prejudices and problems we have today. We can be custodians of what they produced and marvel at Anasazi ingenuity, but the ultimate joy of Mesa Verde is that every visitor can let imagination predominate.

Located in Fewkes Canyon, Oak Tree House contains an unusual mud and twig wall in the back of the alcove. It is a throwback to an earlier construction technique.

interested in them for their dollar value. So many areas are being ravaged by this greed. Laws such as the Archaeological Resources Protection Act are only partially successful in controlling the plundering of America's archaeological sites.

Mesa Verde is an example of foresight in artifact preservation. Its 52,080 acres are safeguarded to national park status. Park rangers try to impress on visitors the importance of leaving potsherds or other artifacts where they find them. Children are thrilled to spot a potsherd and know that it is hundreds of years old. They are more likely to look at it and leave it where they found it if a ranger explains how other children can have the same experience. Children truly do learn to appreciate what national parks provide, carrying that message into adulthood.

A Lasting Message

The Anasazi legacy has another lasting message for modern society. In the 1200s they overused the land, depleted the timber resources, and overhunted the wildlife, just as 20th-century people have done. We hear on the news daily about critical pollution problems, ozone depletion, and overpopulation. As we look at what happened to the Anasazi, perhaps it will be a lesson to us for the future. History does repeat itself, and Mesa Verde is a place to contemplate our wants and needs. If only one visitor in ten takes this message to heart, Mesa Verde is educating thousands of people every year. Give thanks to the Anasazi—their spirit is still with us!

▲ **A** *seasonal ranger gives a guided tour of Spruce Tree House.*

Books on national park areas in "The Story Behind the Scenery" series are: Acadia, Alcatraz Island, Arches, Big Bend, Biscayne, Blue Ridge Parkway, Bryce Canyon, Canyon de Chelly, Canyonlands, Cape Cod, Capitol Reef, Channel Islands, Civil War Parks, Colonial, Crater Lake, Death Valley, Denali, Devils Tower, Dinosaur, Everglades, Fort Clatsop, Gettysburg, Glacier, Glen Canyon-Lake Powell, Grand Canyon, Grand Canyon-North Rim, Grand Teton, Great Smoky Mountains, Haleakala, Hawaii Volcanoes, Independence, Lake Mead-Hoover Dam, Lassen Volcanic, Lincoln Parks, Mammoth Cave, Mesa Verde, Mount Rainier, Mount Rushmore, National Park Service, National Seashores, North Cascades, Olympic, Petrified Forest, Redwood, Rocky Mountain, Scotty's Castle, Sequoia & Kings Canyon, Shenandoah, Statue of Liberty, Theodore Roosevelt, Virgin Islands, Yellowstone, Yosemite, Zion.

Additional books in "The Story Behind the Scenery" series are: Big Sur, Colorado Plateau, Columbia River Gorge, Fire: A Force of Nature, Grand Circle Adventure, John Wesley Powell, Kauai, Lake Tahoe, Las Vegas, Lewis & Clark, Maui, Monument Valley, Mormon Temple Square, Mormon Trail, Mount St. Helens, Nevada's Red Rock Canyon, Nevada's Valley of Fire, Oregon Trail, Oregon Trail Center, Santa Catalina, Santa Fe Trail, Sharks, Sonoran Desert, U.S. Virgin Islands, Water: A Gift of Nature, Whales.

A companion series of national park areas is the NEW: "in pictures...The Continuing Story." This series has **Translation Packages**, providing each title with a complete text both in English and, individually, a second language, German, French, or Japanese. Selected titles in both this series and our other books are available in up to five additional languages. **Call (800-626-9673), fax (702-433-3420), or write to the address below.**

Published by KC Publications, 3245 E. Patrick Ln., Suite A, Las Vegas, NV 89120.

▷ ***I**nside back cover: The setting sun glows in a wintry sky over a Sun Temple kiva*
Photo by Fred Hirschmann

▷ ***B**ack cover: Sun Temple is a favorite spot for reliving a memorable day*
Photo by Terry Donnelly

Created, Designed and Published in the U.S.A.
Printed by Dong-A Publishing and Printing, Seoul, Korea
Color Separations by Kedia/Kwangyangsa Co., Ltd.